Thank you very much for reading this book.

Title: Fractured Bonds

Subtitle: Shattered Connections in a World Where Trust Is a Fragile Echo

Series: Echoes of the Trustless Dawn: Unveiling Humanity's Journey in a World Without Faith

Author: Maxwell J. Aromano

Table of Contents

Introduction 6

Shattered Alliances.....................................6

The Resilience of Discord 8

The Fragile Foundations 11

Chapter 1: Strained Friendships 15

Explore friendships strained by the trustless society. 15

Characters grapple with challenges to their loyalty. 19

Examine the impact of transparent systems on the dynamics of friendship......................................22

Foreshadow conflicts arising from fractured bonds. 25

Chapter 2: Familial Fractures 27

Unravel the strains on families in the trustless world.........27

Characters face challenges to familial bonds.....................30

Explore how transparent systems affect family structures and relationships..................................33

Illustrate the emotional toll of living in a society where trust is replaced by technology........................36

Chapter 3: Romantic Alliances in Disarray 39

Explore challenges to romantic relationships in the trustless era. 39

Characters navigate the complexities of love in a transparent society. 42

Illustrate the emotional toll on romantic connections.........45

Foreshadow conflicts and dilemmas arising from fractured romantic alliances. 48

Chapter 4: Factions in Turmoil **51**

Delve into internal conflicts within factions of the trustless society. 51

Examine power struggles and fractures within ideological groups. 54

Introduce characters caught in the turmoil of factional disputes. 57

Explore the impact of distrust on alliances within and between factions. 60

Chapter 5: Navigating Political Landscape **64**

Explore characters navigating the shifting political landscape. 64

Examine the consequences of internal strife on the governance of the trustless society. 67

Characters face challenges as they try to maintain political stability. 70

Highlight the fragile foundations of the political structures in the trustless world. 73

Chapter 6: Echoes of Resilience **76**

Illustrate the resilience of the human spirit amidst fractured bonds. 76

Characters find strength in unexpected places. 79

Explore the ways individuals cope with the challenges of a trustless society. 82

Foreshadow the potential for renewal and rebuilding 85

Chapter 7: The Lure of New Connections **88**

Explore characters seeking new connections in the trustless society. 88

Examine the allure of forging bonds in a world driven by technology. 91

Characters question the nature of trust in these emerging connections. 94

Set the stage for the exploration of rebuilding trust in unexpected ways. 97

Conclusion **100**

Summarize key events and developments in "Fractured Bonds." 100

Reflect on the characters' journeys amidst shattered alliances. 104

Pose lingering questions and set the stage for the continuation of the series. 107

Glossary **110**

Potential References **113**

Introduction
Shattered Alliances

In a world where trust is a fragile echo, where the very fabric of society is woven with threads of uncertainty, we find ourselves navigating through a landscape of shattered alliances. Welcome to a realm where the bonds that once held us together have been fractured by the relentless march of technology and the erosion of trust.

Within this trustless society, alliances that were once thought unbreakable now lie in ruins, scattered remnants of what once was. The foundations upon which these alliances were built have crumbled, leaving behind a landscape littered with the debris of broken promises and shattered dreams.

In the wake of this destruction, we are left to ponder the consequences of such fractured alliances. What happens when the ties that bind us together are severed, when the bonds of friendship, family, and love are torn asunder? How do we navigate through a world where trust is a scarce commodity, where every interaction is tinged with suspicion and doubt?

The repercussions of these shattered alliances reverberate throughout society, touching every aspect of our lives. From the political arena to the intimate sphere of personal relationships, no corner of our world remains untouched by the specter of mistrust.

Yet amidst the chaos and uncertainty, there is also resilience. For even in the face of adversity, humanity has a remarkable ability to adapt and persevere. It is this resilience that we must call upon as we confront the challenges posed by our trustless society.

In the chapters that follow, we will explore the myriad ways in which fractured alliances manifest themselves in our world. From strained friendships to familial discord, from romantic entanglements to political upheaval, we will delve deep into the heart of our fractured society, seeking to understand the forces that drive us apart and the bonds that hold us together.

But amidst the darkness, there is also hope. For just as alliances can be shattered, so too can they be rebuilt. It is in this spirit of renewal and redemption that we must approach the challenges that lie ahead. For only by confronting the fractures in our society can we hope to mend the bonds that unite us and forge a brighter future for all.

The Resilience of Discord

In a world where trust is a fragile echo, where the very fabric of society is woven with threads of uncertainty, we find ourselves navigating through a landscape of shattered alliances. Welcome to a realm where the bonds that once held us together have been fractured by the relentless march of technology and the erosion of trust.

Amidst the chaos and turmoil of our trustless society, there exists a paradoxical resilience—a resilience born from the very discord that threatens to tear us apart. It is in the midst of shattered alliances that we discover the strength to endure, the courage to persevere, and the determination to rebuild.

In the face of adversity, discord becomes not a sign of weakness, but a testament to our resilience. It is through conflict and strife that we are forced to confront the limitations of our trustless society, to challenge the status quo, and to seek out new paths forward.

For it is only by embracing discord that we can hope to find resolution. In the crucible of conflict, ideas clash, perspectives collide, and new truths emerge. It is through the friction of opposing forces that we are able to refine our understanding of the world around us, to question our assumptions, and to discover new possibilities.

But resilience is not simply a matter of enduring hardship—it is also a matter of adaptation. In a world where trust is a scarce commodity, we are forced to find new ways of navigating through the complexities of human interaction. We must learn to rely not on blind faith, but on reason, empathy, and collaboration.

And so, even as the bonds of trust are shattered, new connections emerge—connections forged not through blind allegiance, but through shared experiences, mutual respect, and a common desire for a better future. It is in these moments of connection that we find hope, for they remind us that even in the darkest of times, the human spirit remains unbroken.

In the chapters that follow, we will explore the many facets of this resilience of discord. From the internal struggles of individuals to the broader conflicts that engulf society, we will delve deep into the heart of our fractured world, seeking to understand the forces that drive us apart and the bonds that hold us together.

But amidst the chaos and uncertainty, there is also opportunity. For in the cracks and crevices of our broken society, there exists the potential for renewal and transformation. It is in these moments of upheaval that we have the chance to redefine ourselves, to challenge the norms that have held us back, and to create a new world—one built not on blind trust, but on the resilient foundation of human connection.

The Fragile Foundations

In a world where trust is a fragile echo, where the very fabric of society is woven with threads of uncertainty, we find ourselves navigating through a landscape of shattered alliances. Welcome to a realm where the bonds that once held us together have been fractured by the relentless march of technology and the erosion of trust.

Beneath the surface of our trustless society lies a network of fragile foundations—structures built upon shifting sands, poised precariously on the edge of collapse. These foundations, once solid and steadfast, have been weakened by the erosion of trust, leaving us teetering on the brink of chaos.

At the heart of these fragile foundations lies the fundamental notion of trust—or rather, the lack thereof. In a society where every interaction is mediated by technology, where transparency reigns supreme and privacy is a thing of the past, trust has become a scarce commodity. Without trust, the very pillars upon which our society rests begin to crumble, threatening to bring the entire edifice crashing down.

One such pillar is that of friendship—a bond forged through mutual respect, shared experiences, and a sense of loyalty. In a trustless society, however, even the strongest friendships are tested, strained by the constant pressure of suspicion and doubt. No longer can we rely on the unspoken bonds of trust that once held us together; instead, we must navigate through a landscape fraught with uncertainty, never quite sure if those closest to us can be trusted.

Similarly, the foundations of family are also under siege in our trustless world. Once thought to be unbreakable, the ties that bind us to our loved ones have been strained to the breaking point, as technology infiltrates every aspect of our lives and erodes the bonds of kinship. In a world where every action is scrutinized, where privacy is a thing of the past, how can we maintain the intimacy and trust that are the hallmarks of family life?

And what of romantic relationships, those most intimate of connections? In a trustless society, even love itself becomes suspect, as the boundaries between reality and illusion blur and the very nature of human connection is called into question. Can we truly trust another person with our deepest desires and fears, or are we destined to remain forever alone, adrift in a sea of uncertainty?

But perhaps most alarming of all is the fragility of our political foundations. In a world where power is concentrated in the hands of the few, where transparency is a facade and corruption runs rampant, how can we hope to maintain any semblance of stability? The very institutions that were meant to safeguard our freedoms have been co-opted by those who seek to control us, leaving us powerless to resist.

Yet amidst the chaos and uncertainty, there is also hope. For just as our foundations have been weakened by the erosion of trust, so too can they be strengthened by its renewal. It is in the cracks and crevices of our broken society that the seeds of change are sown, waiting to take root and blossom into something new and beautiful.

In the chapters that follow, we will explore the many ways in which our fragile foundations are tested and ultimately transformed. From the strained friendships of individuals to the tumultuous political landscape of our society, we will delve deep into the heart of our fractured world, seeking to understand the forces that drive us apart and the bonds that hold us together.

But amidst the chaos and uncertainty, there is also opportunity. For in the midst of destruction lies the potential for creation, and in the ashes of our broken society lies the seeds of a new beginning. It is in these moments of upheaval that we have the chance to redefine ourselves, to challenge the norms that have held us back, and to create a new world—one built not on the fragile foundations of mistrust, but on the solid bedrock of human connection.

Chapter 1: Strained Friendships

Explore friendships strained by the trustless society.

In the trustless society that we inhabit, friendships, once considered bastions of trust and loyalty, have become fraught with uncertainty and suspicion. As technology permeates every aspect of our lives, we find ourselves grappling with the consequences of transparent systems on the dynamics of friendship. In this chapter, we delve into the intricate web of strained friendships, exploring the myriad ways in which trust is eroded and bonds are tested in our trustless world.

In the bustling metropolis of New City, where the gleaming skyscrapers reach towards the heavens and the streets teem with life, we find a group of friends navigating the treacherous waters of distrust and deception. Among them is Sarah, a young woman with a penchant for adventure and a fierce loyalty to her friends. But as the cracks in their friendship begin to widen, Sarah finds herself questioning the very foundation upon which their bond was built.

At the heart of their discord lies the omnipresent specter of technology, which has infiltrated every aspect of their lives, from their social interactions to their most intimate moments. In a world where every conversation is recorded and every action is scrutinized, trust becomes a scarce commodity, and friendships are tested to their breaking point.

As Sarah and her friends grapple with the challenges posed by the trustless society, they find themselves caught in a web of suspicion and doubt. What once seemed like innocent banter now takes on a sinister tone, as every word is weighed and every gesture is scrutinized for signs of betrayal.

But amidst the chaos and uncertainty, there is also resilience. For even as their friendship is strained to its breaking point, Sarah and her friends find solace in the bonds that unite them. Though trust may be elusive, their loyalty to one another remains unwavering, a beacon of hope in a world shrouded in darkness.

Characters grapple with challenges to their loyalty.

As Sarah and her friends confront the challenges posed by the trustless society, they find themselves grappling with questions of loyalty and betrayal. What does it mean to be loyal to a friend in a world where trust is a scarce commodity? How far are they willing to go to protect the bonds that unite them?

For Sarah, the answers are not easy to come by. As she watches her friends succumb to the temptations of distrust and deception, she finds herself torn between loyalty to her friends and loyalty to herself. But as the stakes continue to rise, Sarah realizes that the true test of friendship lies not in blind loyalty, but in the courage to confront the truth, no matter how painful it may be.

Examine the impact of transparent systems on the dynamics of friendship.

In the world of New City, where every interaction is monitored and every action is recorded, the dynamics of friendship are irrevocably altered. Gone are the days of spontaneous outings and intimate conversations; in their place are carefully curated interactions and calculated displays of loyalty.

As Sarah and her friends navigate this brave new world, they find themselves struggling to maintain the authenticity of their friendships in the face of constant scrutiny. What once felt like genuine connections now seem hollow and superficial, as the specter of distrust hangs heavy in the air.

But amidst the chaos and uncertainty, there is also opportunity. For in the crucible of adversity, true friendships are forged, their bonds strengthened by the trials they face together. As Sarah and her friends come to realize, it is not the absence of trust that defines their friendship, but rather their willingness to confront the challenges posed by the trustless society head-on.

Foreshadow conflicts arising from fractured bonds.

As the sun sets over the skyline of New City, casting long shadows over the bustling streets below, Sarah and her friends find themselves standing at a crossroads. Though their friendship has been tested and strained by the challenges of the trustless society, they know that the true test is yet to come.

For in the shadows lurks a darkness far greater than they could have imagined, a darkness that threatens to consume them all. As Sarah and her friends brace themselves for the storm that lies ahead, they know that their bonds will be tested like never before. But amidst the chaos and uncertainty, they also know that their friendship is stronger than any force the trustless society can muster.

And so, as they stand together in the gathering darkness, Sarah and her friends vow to confront the challenges that lie ahead with courage and determination. For though the road may be long and fraught with peril, they know that as long as they have each other, they can overcome anything that stands in their way.

In the trustless society that we inhabit, friendships, once considered bastions of trust and loyalty, have become fraught with uncertainty and suspicion. As technology permeates every aspect of our lives, we find ourselves grappling with the consequences of transparent systems on the dynamics of friendship. In this chapter, we delve into the intricate web of strained friendships, exploring the myriad ways in which trust is eroded and bonds are tested in our trustless world.

Amidst the gleaming skyscrapers and bustling streets of New City, a group of friends navigates the complexities of their relationships in a world where trust is a scarce commodity. Among them is Alex, a fiercely loyal friend who prides himself on his unwavering commitment to those he holds dear. But as the cracks in their friendship begin to widen, Alex finds himself grappling with challenges to his loyalty that threaten to tear their bond apart.

At the heart of their discord lies the omnipresent specter of technology, which has infiltrated every aspect of their lives, from their social interactions to their most intimate moments. In a world where every conversation is recorded and every action is scrutinized, trust becomes a scarce commodity, and friendships are tested to their breaking point.

As Alex and his friends confront the challenges posed by the trustless society, they find themselves caught in a web of suspicion and doubt. What once seemed like innocent banter now takes on a sinister tone, as every word is weighed and every gesture is scrutinized for signs of betrayal.

But amidst the chaos and uncertainty, there is also resilience. For even as their friendship is strained to its breaking point, Alex and his friends find solace in the bonds that unite them. Though trust may be elusive, their loyalty to one another remains unwavering, a beacon of hope in a world shrouded in darkness.

As Alex grapples with challenges to his loyalty, he finds himself wrestling with questions of identity and self-worth. What does it mean to be loyal to a friend in a world where trust is a scarce commodity? How far is he willing to go to protect the bonds that unite them?

For Alex, the answers are not easy to come by. As he watches his friends succumb to the temptations of distrust and deception, he finds himself torn between loyalty to his friends and loyalty to himself. But as the stakes continue to rise, Alex realizes that the true test of friendship lies not in blind loyalty, but in the courage to confront the truth, no matter how painful it may be.

As Alex grapples with these challenges, he is forced to confront his own beliefs and values, questioning the very foundation upon which his friendship with his friends was built. But amidst the chaos and uncertainty, there is also opportunity. For in the crucible of adversity, true friendships are forged, their bonds strengthened by the trials they face together.

As Alex and his friends come to realize, it is not the absence of trust that defines their friendship, but rather their willingness to confront the challenges posed by the trustless society head-on. And so, as they stand together in the gathering darkness, they vow to confront the challenges that lie ahead with courage and determination. For though the road may be long and fraught with peril, they know that as long as they have each other, they can overcome anything that stands in their way.

Examine the impact of transparent systems on the dynamics of friendship.

In the trustless society that we inhabit, friendships, once considered bastions of trust and loyalty, have become fraught with uncertainty and suspicion. As technology permeates every aspect of our lives, we find ourselves grappling with the consequences of transparent systems on the dynamics of friendship. In this chapter, we delve into the intricate web of strained friendships, exploring the myriad ways in which trust is eroded and bonds are tested in our trustless world.

In the heart of New City, where the digital pulse of society beats incessantly, friendships once thought unassailable are now subject to the scrutiny of transparent systems. No longer can conversations be held in private, nor actions taken without observation. Every word spoken, every gesture made, is recorded and analyzed, casting a pall of suspicion over even the most innocent of interactions.

For Jenna and her friends, the impact of these transparent systems on their friendships is palpable. Once inseparable, they now find themselves navigating a minefield of distrust and uncertainty, their every move scrutinized for signs of betrayal. What once felt like genuine connections now seem hollow and superficial, as the specter of mistrust looms large over their once-unshakeable bond.

As Jenna and her friends grapple with the challenges posed by transparent systems, they find themselves questioning the very nature of their friendships. Can true intimacy exist in a world where every conversation is monitored and every action analyzed? Can genuine trust be fostered when every interaction is subject to the scrutiny of an unseen observer?

But amidst the chaos and uncertainty, there is also resilience. For even as their friendships are strained to the breaking point, Jenna and her friends find solace in the bonds that unite them. Though trust may be elusive, their loyalty to one another remains unwavering, a testament to the enduring power of human connection in the face of adversity.

As Jenna examines the impact of transparent systems on the dynamics of her friendships, she is forced to confront uncomfortable truths about the nature of trust and intimacy in the digital age. No longer can she take her friendships for granted; every interaction must be carefully calibrated, every word weighed for its potential consequences. And yet, amidst the chaos and uncertainty, Jenna finds hope.

For in the crucible of adversity, true friendships are forged, their bonds strengthened by the trials they face together. As Jenna and her friends come to realize, it is not the absence of trust that defines their friendship, but rather their willingness to confront the challenges posed by transparent systems head-on.

And so, as they stand together in the gathering darkness, Jenna and her friends vow to confront the challenges that lie ahead with courage and determination. For though the road may be long and fraught with peril, they know that as long as they have each other, they can overcome anything that stands in their way.

In the trustless society that we inhabit, friendships, once considered bastions of trust and loyalty, have become fraught with uncertainty and suspicion. As technology permeates every aspect of our lives, we find ourselves grappling with the consequences of transparent systems on the dynamics of friendship. In this chapter, we delve into the intricate web of strained friendships, exploring the myriad ways in which trust is eroded and bonds are tested in our trustless world.

As Sarah and her friends navigate the turbulent waters of their strained friendships, ominous clouds gather on the horizon, foreshadowing conflicts that threaten to tear their bonds apart. Though they may cling to the hope of reconciliation, the specter of mistrust looms large over their once-unshakeable alliance.

In the shadows of New City, unseen forces conspire to sow discord among Sarah and her friends, pitting them against one another in a desperate struggle for survival. What once seemed like innocent disagreements now take on a sinister tone, as alliances shift and loyalties are tested in the crucible of mistrust.

But amidst the chaos and uncertainty, there is also opportunity. For in the darkness, new alliances are forged, their bonds strengthened by the trials they face together. Though the road ahead may be fraught with danger, Sarah and her friends know that as long as they stand united, they can overcome any obstacle that stands in their way.

As Sarah confronts the conflicts that lie ahead, she is forced to confront uncomfortable truths about the nature of friendship and loyalty in the trustless society. No longer can she rely on the bonds of trust that once held her friendships together; every interaction must be approached with caution, every word weighed for its potential consequences.

And yet, amidst the chaos and uncertainty, Sarah finds hope. For in the crucible of adversity, true friendships are forged, their bonds strengthened by the trials they face together. As Sarah and her friends come to realize, it is not the absence of trust that defines their friendship, but rather their willingness to confront the challenges posed by fractured bonds head-on.

And so, as they stand together in the gathering darkness, Sarah and her friends vow to confront the conflicts that lie ahead with courage and determination. For though the road may be long and fraught with peril, they know that as long as they have each other, they can overcome anything that stands in their way.

Chapter 2: Familial Fractures
Unravel the strains on families in the trustless world.

In the trustless society that we inhabit, families, once considered pillars of support and stability, have become ensnared in a web of mistrust and discord. As technology infiltrates every aspect of our lives, we find ourselves grappling with the consequences of transparent systems on the dynamics of family relationships. In this chapter, we unravel the strains on families in the trustless world, exploring the myriad ways in which trust is eroded and bonds are tested within the familial unit.

Amidst the towering skyscrapers and bustling streets of New City, the Tran family finds itself navigating the treacherous waters of familial discord. Once bound by the ties of blood and kinship, they now find themselves torn apart by the relentless march of technology and the erosion of trust.

At the heart of their discord lies the omnipresent specter of transparent systems, which have infiltrated every aspect of their lives, from their most intimate conversations to their most private moments. No longer can they rely on the sanctity of family ties; every interaction is scrutinized, every action analyzed for signs of betrayal.

As the Tran family grapples with the challenges posed by the trustless world, they find themselves questioning the very foundation upon which their familial bonds were built. Can true intimacy exist in a world where every word is recorded and every action monitored? Can genuine trust be fostered when every interaction is subject to the scrutiny of an unseen observer?

But amidst the chaos and uncertainty, there is also resilience. For even as their familial bonds are strained to the breaking point, the Tran family finds solace in the bonds that unite them. Though trust may be elusive, their love for one another remains unwavering, a beacon of hope in a world shrouded in darkness.

As the Trans unravel the strains on their family in the trustless world, they are forced to confront uncomfortable truths about the nature of trust and intimacy in the digital age. No longer can they take their familial bonds for granted; every interaction must be carefully calibrated, every word weighed for its potential consequences.

And yet, amidst the chaos and uncertainty, the Tran family finds hope. For in the crucible of adversity, true familial bonds are forged, their strength tested by the trials they face together. As the Trans come to realize, it is not the absence of trust that defines their family, but rather their willingness to confront the challenges posed by the trustless world head-on.

And so, as they stand together in the gathering darkness, the Tran family vows to confront the strains that lie ahead with courage and determination. For though the road may be long and fraught with peril, they know that as long as they have each other, they can overcome anything that stands in their way.

Characters face challenges to familial bonds.

In the trustless society that we inhabit, families, once considered pillars of support and stability, have become ensnared in a web of mistrust and discord. As technology infiltrates every aspect of our lives, we find ourselves grappling with the consequences of transparent systems on the dynamics of family relationships. In this chapter, we unravel the strains on families in the trustless world, exploring the myriad ways in which trust is eroded and bonds are tested within the familial unit.

In the heart of New City, amidst the hum of activity and the glow of neon lights, the Leung family struggles to maintain their once-unshakeable bonds in the face of mounting challenges. For Mei Leung, the matriarch of the family, the erosion of trust within her familial unit is a source of deep anguish and sorrow.

As Mei grapples with the challenges posed by the trustless world, she finds herself questioning the very foundation upon which her familial bonds were built. Can true intimacy exist in a world where every word is recorded and every action monitored? Can genuine trust be fostered when every interaction is subject to the scrutiny of an unseen observer?

For Mei, the answers are not easy to come by. As she watches her family drift further apart, torn asunder by the relentless march of technology and the erosion of trust, she feels a profound sense of loss and despair. No longer can she rely on the sanctity of family ties; every interaction is fraught with tension and uncertainty, every word weighed for its potential consequences.

But amidst the chaos and uncertainty, there is also resilience. For even as their familial bonds are strained to the breaking point, the Leung family finds solace in the bonds that unite them. Though trust may be elusive, their love for one another remains unwavering, a beacon of hope in a world shrouded in darkness.

As Mei and her family face challenges to their familial bonds, they are forced to confront uncomfortable truths about the nature of trust and intimacy in the digital age. No longer can they take their familial bonds for granted; every interaction must be carefully calibrated, every word weighed for its potential consequences.

And yet, amidst the chaos and uncertainty, the Leung family finds hope. For in the crucible of adversity, true familial bonds are forged, their strength tested by the trials they face together. As Mei and her family come to realize, it is not the absence of trust that defines their family, but rather their willingness to confront the challenges posed by the trustless world head-on.

As they stand together in the gathering darkness, the Leung family vows to confront the strains that lie ahead with courage and determination. For though the road may be long and fraught with peril, they know that as long as they have each other, they can overcome anything that stands in their way.

Explore how transparent systems affect family structures and relationships.

In the trustless society that we inhabit, families, once considered pillars of support and stability, have become ensnared in a web of mistrust and discord. As technology infiltrates every aspect of our lives, we find ourselves grappling with the consequences of transparent systems on the dynamics of family relationships. In this chapter, we unravel the strains on families in the trustless world, exploring the myriad ways in which trust is eroded and bonds are tested within the familial unit.

In the bustling metropolis of New City, the Tran family sits down for dinner, the glow of their screens casting eerie shadows across the room. Each member of the family is engrossed in their own digital world, their faces illuminated by the soft glow of their devices. Gone are the days of family meals and meaningful conversations; in their place are isolated individuals, connected only by the thin threads of technology.

For the Trans, like many families in the trustless world, technology has become both a blessing and a curse. On one hand, it offers unprecedented convenience and connectivity, allowing them to communicate with ease and efficiency. But on the other hand, it has also eroded the intimacy and closeness that once defined their familial relationships.

No longer can they rely on face-to-face interactions to foster trust and understanding; instead, they must navigate the complexities of digital communication, where every word is subject to misinterpretation and every action is scrutinized for signs of deception.

As the Trans struggle to adapt to the challenges posed by transparent systems, they find themselves grappling with questions of identity and belonging. What does it mean to be a family in a world where technology reigns supreme? Can true intimacy exist in a world where every interaction is mediated by screens and algorithms?

For the Trans, the answers are not easy to come by. As they navigate the murky waters of digital communication, they find themselves longing for the simplicity and authenticity of face-to-face interaction. No longer can they rely on the familiar rhythms of family life; instead, they must navigate a virtual landscape fraught with uncertainty and mistrust.

But amidst the chaos and uncertainty, there is also opportunity. For even as their familial bonds are strained to the breaking point, the Trans find solace in the bonds that unite them. Though trust may be elusive, their love for one another remains unwavering, a beacon of hope in a world shrouded in darkness.

As the Trans explore how transparent systems affect their family structures and relationships, they are forced to confront uncomfortable truths about the nature of trust and intimacy in the digital age. No longer can they take their familial bonds for granted; every interaction must be carefully calibrated, every word weighed for its potential consequences.

And yet, amidst the chaos and uncertainty, the Trans find hope. For in the crucible of adversity, true familial bonds are forged, their strength tested by the trials they face together. As the Trans come to realize, it is not the absence of trust that defines their family, but rather their willingness to confront the challenges posed by transparent systems head-on.

As they stand together in the gathering darkness, the Trans vow to confront the strains that lie ahead with courage and determination. For though the road may be long and fraught with peril, they know that as long as they have each other, they can overcome anything that stands in their way.

Illustrate the emotional toll of living in a society where trust is replaced by technology.

In the trustless society that we inhabit, families, once considered pillars of support and stability, have become ensnared in a web of mistrust and discord. As technology infiltrates every aspect of our lives, we find ourselves grappling with the consequences of transparent systems on the dynamics of family relationships. In this chapter, we unravel the strains on families in the trustless world, exploring the myriad ways in which trust is eroded and bonds are tested within the familial unit.

In the tranquil suburbs of New City, the Wang family gathers for their weekly movie night, a tradition that once brought them together in laughter and joy. But tonight, there is an unspoken tension in the air, a palpable sense of unease that hangs heavy over the room. For the Wangs, like many families in the trustless world, technology has become both a blessing and a curse.

As they settle in to watch their movie, each member of the family is engrossed in their own digital world, their faces illuminated by the soft glow of their devices. Gone are the days of shared laughter and meaningful conversations; in their place are isolated individuals, connected only by the thin threads of technology.

For the Wangs, the emotional toll of living in a society where trust is replaced by technology is all too real. No longer can they rely on face-to-face interactions to foster trust and understanding; instead, they must navigate the complexities of digital communication, where every word is subject to misinterpretation and every action is scrutinized for signs of deception.

As the Wangs struggle to adapt to the challenges posed by transparent systems, they find themselves grappling with a myriad of emotions. Anger, frustration, and resentment bubble to the surface, threatening to tear their already fragile bonds apart. No longer can they rely on the familiar rhythms of family life; instead, they must navigate a virtual landscape fraught with uncertainty and mistrust.

But amidst the chaos and uncertainty, there is also opportunity. For even as their familial bonds are strained to the breaking point, the Wangs find solace in the bonds that unite them. Though trust may be elusive, their love for one another remains unwavering, a beacon of hope in a world shrouded in darkness.

As the Wangs illustrate the emotional toll of living in a society where trust is replaced by technology, they are forced to confront uncomfortable truths about the nature of trust and intimacy in the digital age. No longer can they take their familial bonds for granted; every interaction must be carefully calibrated, every word weighed for its potential consequences.

And yet, amidst the chaos and uncertainty, the Wangs find hope. For in the crucible of adversity, true familial bonds are forged, their strength tested by the trials they face together. As the Wangs come to realize, it is not the absence of trust that defines their family, but rather their willingness to confront the challenges posed by transparent systems head-on.

As they stand together in the gathering darkness, the Wangs vow to confront the strains that lie ahead with courage and determination. For though the road may be long and fraught with peril, they know that as long as they have each other, they can overcome anything that stands in their way.

Chapter 3: Romantic Alliances in Disarray
Explore challenges to romantic relationships in the trustless era.

In the trustless society that we inhabit, even the most intimate of connections are not immune to the erosion of trust and the pervasiveness of technology. Romantic relationships, once seen as the epitome of trust and devotion, find themselves ensnared in a web of suspicion and uncertainty. In this chapter, we explore the challenges faced by romantic alliances in the trustless era, delving into the complexities of love in a world where trust is a fragile echo.

In the heart of New City, amidst the hustle and bustle of daily life, we find Mia and Jake, a young couple navigating the complexities of love in the trustless era. Once inseparable, they now find themselves grappling with the challenges posed by transparent systems and the erosion of trust.

At the heart of their disarray lies the omnipresent specter of technology, which has infiltrated every aspect of their relationship, from their most intimate moments to their most trivial disagreements. No longer can they rely on the sanctity of their love to bridge the divide between them; instead, they must navigate a minefield of suspicion and uncertainty, where every word is weighed and every action scrutinized for signs of betrayal.

As Mia and Jake confront the challenges posed by the trustless era, they find themselves questioning the very foundation upon which their relationship was built. Can true intimacy exist in a world where every interaction is monitored and every action analyzed? Can genuine trust be fostered when every gesture is subject to the scrutiny of an unseen observer?

For Mia and Jake, the answers are not easy to come by. As they struggle to navigate the complexities of their relationship in the trustless era, they find themselves grappling with a myriad of emotions. Anger, frustration, and resentment bubble to the surface, threatening to tear their already fragile bond apart.

But amidst the chaos and uncertainty, there is also resilience. For even as their romantic alliance is tested to its breaking point, Mia and Jake find solace in the love that unites them. Though trust may be elusive, their devotion to one another remains unwavering, a beacon of hope in a world shrouded in darkness.

As Mia and Jake explore the challenges to their romantic relationship in the trustless era, they are forced to confront uncomfortable truths about the nature of love and intimacy in the digital age. No longer can they take their relationship for granted; every interaction must be carefully calibrated, every word weighed for its potential consequences.

And yet, amidst the chaos and uncertainty, Mia and Jake find hope. For in the crucible of adversity, true love is forged, its strength tested by the trials they face together. As Mia and Jake come to realize, it is not the absence of trust that defines their relationship, but rather their willingness to confront the challenges posed by the trustless era head-on.

As they stand together in the gathering darkness, Mia and Jake vow to confront the challenges that lie ahead with courage and determination. For though the road may be long and fraught with peril, they know that as long as they have each other, they can overcome anything that stands in their way.

Characters navigate the complexities of love in a transparent society.

In a world where trust is a scarce commodity and transparency reigns supreme, even the most intimate of connections are subject to scrutiny and doubt. Romantic relationships, once considered sanctuaries of trust and devotion, find themselves navigating treacherous waters in the trustless era. In this chapter, we delve into the complexities of love in a transparent society, exploring how characters grapple with the challenges posed by the erosion of trust and the omnipresence of technology.

In the heart of New City, amidst the gleaming skyscrapers and bustling streets, we find Sophia and Marcus, two individuals caught in the throes of a tumultuous romance. Once, their love burned bright and unyielding, a beacon of hope in a world shrouded in darkness. But as the specter of mistrust looms large over their relationship, they find themselves navigating a maze of uncertainty and doubt.

For Sophia and Marcus, the complexities of love in a transparent society are all too real. No longer can they rely on the sanctity of their bond to weather the storms that assail them; instead, they must confront the harsh realities of a world where every interaction is scrutinized and every gesture analyzed for signs of betrayal.

As they navigate the treacherous waters of their relationship, Sophia and Marcus find themselves grappling with a myriad of emotions. Fear, insecurity, and doubt threaten to tear them apart, casting a shadow over the love that once bound them together. Can their relationship withstand the relentless onslaught of mistrust and suspicion, or are they destined to become casualties of the trustless era?

But amidst the chaos and uncertainty, there is also resilience. For even as their love is tested to its breaking point, Sophia and Marcus find solace in the moments of connection that still bind them together. Though trust may be elusive, their devotion to one another remains unwavering, a glimmer of hope in a world consumed by darkness.

As Sophia and Marcus navigate the complexities of love in a transparent society, they are forced to confront uncomfortable truths about the nature of intimacy and connection in the digital age. No longer can they take their relationship for granted; every interaction must be approached with caution, every word weighed for its potential consequences.

And yet, amidst the chaos and uncertainty, Sophia and Marcus find hope. For in the crucible of adversity, true love is forged, its strength tested by the trials they face together. As they come to realize, it is not the absence of trust that defines their relationship, but rather their willingness to confront the challenges posed by the trustless era head-on.

As they stand together in the gathering darkness, Sophia and Marcus vow to confront the complexities of love in a transparent society with courage and determination. For though the road may be long and fraught with peril, they know that as long as they have each other, they can overcome anything that stands in their way.

Illustrate the emotional toll on romantic connections.

In the tumultuous landscape of the trustless society, where transparency reigns supreme and trust is a fragile echo, romantic relationships are subjected to unprecedented challenges. In this chapter, we delve into the emotional toll inflicted upon romantic connections as characters grapple with the erosion of trust and the complexities of love in a world driven by technology and suspicion.

In the heart of New City, amidst the cacophony of urban life, we find Emma and Daniel, a couple navigating the rocky terrain of their relationship in the trustless era. Once, their love was a source of strength and comfort, a beacon of hope in a world fraught with uncertainty. But as the specter of mistrust looms large over their romance, they find themselves ensnared in a web of doubt and insecurity.

For Emma and Daniel, the emotional toll of living in a society where trust is replaced by technology is profound and far-reaching. No longer can they rely on the security of their bond to weather the storms that assail them; instead, they must confront the harsh realities of a world where every interaction is scrutinized and every gesture analyzed for signs of betrayal.

As they navigate the treacherous waters of their relationship, Emma and Daniel find themselves grappling with a myriad of emotions. Fear, insecurity, and doubt threaten to consume them, casting a shadow over the love that once bound them together. Can their relationship withstand the relentless onslaught of mistrust and suspicion, or are they destined to become casualties of the trustless era?

But amidst the chaos and uncertainty, there is also resilience. For even as their love is tested to its breaking point, Emma and Daniel find solace in the moments of connection that still bind them together. Though trust may be elusive, their devotion to one another remains unwavering, a glimmer of hope in a world consumed by darkness.

As Emma and Daniel illustrate the emotional toll on romantic connections, they are forced to confront uncomfortable truths about the nature of intimacy and connection in the digital age. No longer can they take their relationship for granted; every interaction must be approached with caution, every word weighed for its potential consequences.

And yet, amidst the chaos and uncertainty, Emma and Daniel find hope. For in the crucible of adversity, true love is forged, its strength tested by the trials they face together. As they come to realize, it is not the absence of trust that defines their relationship, but rather their willingness to confront the challenges posed by the trustless era head-on.

As they stand together in the gathering darkness, Emma and Daniel vow to confront the emotional toll on romantic connections with courage and determination. For though the road may be long and fraught with peril, they know that as long as they have each other, they can overcome anything that stands in their way.

Foreshadow conflicts and dilemmas arising from fractured romantic alliances.

In the ever-evolving landscape of the trustless society, where transparency reigns supreme and the bonds of trust are constantly tested, romantic relationships find themselves on shaky ground. In this chapter, we delve into the complexities of love in a world where trust is fragile and technology dominates, exploring how characters navigate the challenges and conflicts that arise from fractured romantic alliances.

In the heart of New City, amidst the hustle and bustle of daily life, we find Alex and Sarah, a couple grappling with the fractures that have begun to appear in their once-solid relationship. Once, their love was a source of strength and comfort, a refuge from the chaos of the world outside. But as the specter of mistrust looms large over their romance, they find themselves on the brink of collapse.

For Alex and Sarah, the conflicts and dilemmas arising from their fractured romantic alliance are manifold. No longer can they rely on the stability of their bond to weather the storms that assail them; instead, they must confront the harsh realities of a world where every interaction is scrutinized and every gesture analyzed for signs of betrayal.

As they navigate the treacherous waters of their relationship, Alex and Sarah find themselves grappling with a myriad of emotions. Fear, insecurity, and doubt threaten to consume them, casting a shadow over the love that once bound them together. Can their relationship withstand the relentless onslaught of mistrust and suspicion, or are they destined to become casualties of the trustless era?

But amidst the chaos and uncertainty, there is also resilience. For even as their love is tested to its breaking point, Alex and Sarah find solace in the moments of connection that still bind them together. Though trust may be elusive, their devotion to one another remains unwavering, a glimmer of hope in a world consumed by darkness.

As Alex and Sarah foreshadow conflicts and dilemmas arising from their fractured romantic alliance, they are forced to confront uncomfortable truths about the nature of intimacy and connection in the digital age. No longer can they take their relationship for granted; every interaction must be approached with caution, every word weighed for its potential consequences.

And yet, amidst the chaos and uncertainty, Alex and Sarah find hope. For in the crucible of adversity, true love is forged, its strength tested by the trials they face together. As they come to realize, it is not the absence of trust that defines their relationship, but rather their willingness to confront the challenges posed by the trustless era head-on.

As they stand together in the gathering darkness, Alex and Sarah vow to confront the conflicts and dilemmas that arise from their fractured romantic alliance with courage and determination. For though the road may be long and fraught with peril, they know that as long as they have each other, they can overcome anything that stands in their way.

Chapter 4: Factions in Turmoil
Delve into internal conflicts within factions of the trustless society.

In the intricate tapestry of the trustless society, where alliances are fragile and power is constantly shifting, factions find themselves embroiled in a constant struggle for dominance. In this chapter, we delve into the internal conflicts that plague factions within the trustless society, exploring the complexities of loyalty and betrayal in a world driven by technology and distrust.

In the heart of New City, amidst the towering skyscrapers and bustling streets, we find the Tech Consortium, one of the most powerful factions in the trustless society, on the brink of collapse. Once united in their pursuit of technological advancement and innovation, internal conflicts threaten to tear them apart from within.

At the heart of their turmoil lies a power struggle between two rival factions within the Tech Consortium, each vying for control over the organization's resources and influence. As tensions escalate and loyalties are tested, members of the Tech Consortium find themselves torn between conflicting allegiances, unsure of whom to trust and where their true loyalties lie.

For the leaders of the rival factions, the internal conflicts within the Tech Consortium represent a threat to their very existence. No longer can they rely on the unity and cohesion that once defined their organization; instead, they must confront the harsh realities of a world where betrayal lurks around every corner and alliances are fleeting.

As the Tech Consortium delves into the depths of their internal conflicts, they find themselves grappling with a myriad of emotions. Anger, resentment, and mistrust threaten to consume them, casting a shadow over the once-unshakeable bonds that united them. Can they overcome their differences and find a way to reconcile their competing interests, or are they doomed to descend into chaos and destruction?

But amidst the chaos and uncertainty, there is also opportunity. For even as the Tech Consortium teeters on the brink of collapse, there are those who see the internal conflicts as a chance for renewal and reinvention. Though trust may be scarce and betrayal may lurk around every corner, the leaders of the Tech Consortium refuse to surrender to despair. Instead, they vow to confront the internal conflicts head-on, determined to emerge stronger and more resilient than ever before.

As the Tech Consortium delves into the internal conflicts that threaten to tear them apart, they are forced to confront uncomfortable truths about the nature of power and loyalty in the trustless society. No longer can they take their alliances for granted; every interaction must be approached with caution, every decision weighed for its potential consequences.

And yet, amidst the chaos and uncertainty, the Tech Consortium finds hope. For in the crucible of adversity, true alliances are forged, their strength tested by the trials they face together. As they come to realize, it is not the absence of conflict that defines their organization, but rather their willingness to confront the internal conflicts head-on and emerge stronger as a result.

As they stand together in the gathering darkness, the Tech Consortium vows to confront the internal conflicts that threaten to tear them apart with courage and determination. For though the road may be long and fraught with peril, they know that as long as they have each other, they can overcome anything that stands in their way.

In the intricate tapestry of the trustless society, where alliances are fragile and power is constantly shifting, factions find themselves embroiled in a constant struggle for dominance. In this chapter, we delve into the internal conflicts that plague factions within the trustless society, exploring the complexities of loyalty and betrayal in a world driven by technology and distrust.

In the heart of New City, amidst the towering skyscrapers and bustling streets, the Order of Transparency stands as a bastion of ideological purity, dedicated to the principles of openness and accountability. But beneath their facade of unity lies a web of power struggles and fractures that threaten to tear the organization apart from within.

At the heart of their turmoil lies a battle for control between two rival factions within the Order of Transparency, each vying for supremacy over the organization's agenda and direction. As tensions escalate and loyalties are tested, members of the Order find themselves torn between conflicting allegiances, unsure of whom to trust and where their true loyalties lie.

For the leaders of the rival factions, the power struggles and fractures within the Order of Transparency represent a threat to their very existence. No longer can they rely on the unity and cohesion that once defined their organization; instead, they must confront the harsh realities of a world where betrayal lurks around every corner and alliances are fleeting.

As the Order of Transparency examines the power struggles and fractures that threaten to tear them apart, they find themselves grappling with a myriad of emotions. Anger, resentment, and mistrust threaten to consume them, casting a shadow over the once-unshakeable bonds that united them. Can they overcome their differences and find a way to reconcile their competing interests, or are they doomed to descend into chaos and destruction?

But amidst the chaos and uncertainty, there is also opportunity. For even as the Order of Transparency teeters on the brink of collapse, there are those who see the internal conflicts as a chance for renewal and reinvention. Though trust may be scarce and betrayal may lurk around every corner, the leaders of the Order refuse to surrender to despair. Instead, they vow to confront the power struggles and fractures head-on, determined to emerge stronger and more resilient than ever before.

As the Order of Transparency examines the power struggles and fractures that threaten to tear them apart, they are forced to confront uncomfortable truths about the nature of power and loyalty in the trustless society. No longer can they take their alliances for granted; every interaction must be approached with caution, every decision weighed for its potential consequences.

And yet, amidst the chaos and uncertainty, the Order of Transparency finds hope. For in the crucible of adversity, true alliances are forged, their strength tested by the trials they face together. As they come to realize, it is not the absence of conflict that defines their organization, but rather their willingness to confront the power struggles and fractures head-on and emerge stronger as a result.

Standing together in the gathering darkness, the Order of Transparency vows to confront the power struggles and fractures that threaten to tear them apart with courage and determination. For though the road may be long and fraught with peril, they know that as long as they have each other, they can overcome anything that stands in their way.

Introduce characters caught in the turmoil of factional disputes.

In the intricate tapestry of the trustless society, where alliances are fragile and power is constantly shifting, factions find themselves embroiled in a constant struggle for dominance. In this chapter, we delve into the internal conflicts that plague factions within the trustless society, exploring the complexities of loyalty and betrayal in a world driven by technology and distrust.

In the heart of New City, amidst the towering skyscrapers and bustling streets, we encounter Ethan and Ava, two individuals whose lives have become entangled in the tumultuous world of factional disputes. Once, they were members of the same faction, united in their shared beliefs and aspirations. But as the factional disputes escalate and loyalties are tested, they find themselves on opposing sides of a bitter conflict.

Ethan, a charismatic leader within the faction, has long been regarded as a voice of reason and moderation. He believes in the power of unity and cooperation, advocating for dialogue and compromise as the keys to resolving the faction's internal conflicts. But as tensions rise and rival factions seek to undermine his authority, he finds himself increasingly isolated and vulnerable.

Ava, on the other hand, is a passionate advocate for radical change within the faction. She believes that compromise is a sign of weakness, and that the only path forward is through bold action and decisive leadership. As the faction's internal disputes intensify, she finds herself at odds with Ethan and his vision for the future, pushing for more radical measures to assert their dominance.

As Ethan and Ava navigate the treacherous waters of factional disputes, they find themselves grappling with a myriad of emotions. Anger, resentment, and mistrust threaten to consume them, casting a shadow over the once-unshakeable bonds that united them. Can they overcome their differences and find a way to reconcile their competing interests, or are they destined to become casualties of the trustless era?

But amidst the chaos and uncertainty, there is also resilience. For even as Ethan and Ava find themselves caught in the turmoil of factional disputes, they refuse to surrender to despair. Instead, they vow to confront the challenges posed by the trustless society head-on, determined to emerge stronger and more resilient than ever before.

As Ethan and Ava grapple with the complexities of factional disputes, they are forced to confront uncomfortable truths about the nature of power and loyalty in the trustless society. No longer can they take their alliances for granted; every interaction must be approached with caution, every decision weighed for its potential consequences.

And yet, amidst the chaos and uncertainty, Ethan and Ava find hope. For in the crucible of adversity, true alliances are forged, their strength tested by the trials they face together. As they come to realize, it is not the absence of conflict that defines their faction, but rather their willingness to confront the challenges posed by factional disputes head-on and emerge stronger as a result.

Standing together in the gathering darkness, Ethan and Ava vow to confront the factional disputes that threaten to tear them apart with courage and determination. For though the road may be long and fraught with peril, they know that as long as they have each other, they can overcome anything that stands in their way.

Explore the impact of distrust on alliances within and between factions.

In the intricate tapestry of the trustless society, where alliances are fragile and power is constantly shifting, factions find themselves embroiled in a constant struggle for dominance. In this chapter, we delve into the internal conflicts that plague factions within the trustless society, exploring the complexities of loyalty and betrayal in a world driven by technology and distrust.

In the heart of New City, amidst the towering skyscrapers and bustling streets, we witness the profound impact of distrust on alliances within and between factions. Once, these factions were united in their pursuit of common goals and shared values. But as mistrust seeps into their ranks, these alliances begin to unravel, torn apart by suspicion and betrayal.

Within the ranks of the Tech Consortium, one of the most powerful factions in the trustless society, distrust runs rampant. Once, the members of the Consortium were bound together by a shared vision of technological progress and innovation. But as rival factions vie for control and influence, trust becomes a scarce commodity, with each member looking over their shoulder, unsure of whom to trust.

As distrust deepens within the Tech Consortium, alliances that were once thought unbreakable begin to crumble. Members who once stood shoulder to shoulder find themselves at odds, their loyalty called into question by those who seek to exploit their vulnerabilities. In the face of this betrayal, trust becomes a precious commodity, hoarded by those who fear the consequences of betrayal.

But it is not just within factions that distrust takes its toll. Between factions, the impact of mistrust is equally profound. Once, alliances between factions were formed out of mutual respect and shared interests. But as distrust spreads like a virus, these alliances begin to fray, torn apart by suspicion and paranoia.

In the heart of New City, the Order of Transparency stands as a beacon of hope in a world consumed by distrust. Once, they were a force for good, dedicated to the principles of openness and accountability. But as mistrust seeps into their ranks, the Order finds itself torn apart by internal conflicts and power struggles.

As distrust spreads like a cancer within and between factions, the very fabric of society begins to unravel. No longer can factions rely on the stability of their alliances to weather the storms that assail them. Instead, they must confront the harsh realities of a world where betrayal lurks around every corner and alliances are fleeting.

And yet, amidst the chaos and uncertainty, there is also resilience. For even as distrust tears at the fabric of society, there are those who refuse to surrender to despair. Instead, they vow to confront the challenges posed by mistrust head-on, determined to rebuild what has been lost and forge new alliances based on mutual respect and understanding.

As factions grapple with the impact of distrust on their alliances, they are forced to confront uncomfortable truths about the nature of power and loyalty in the trustless society. No longer can they take their alliances for granted; every interaction must be approached with caution, every decision weighed for its potential consequences.

And yet, amidst the chaos and uncertainty, there is also hope. For in the crucible of adversity, true alliances are forged, their strength tested by the trials they face together. As factions come to realize, it is not the absence of distrust that defines their alliances, but rather their willingness to confront the challenges posed by mistrust head-on and emerge stronger as a result.

Standing together in the gathering darkness, factions vow to confront the impact of distrust on their alliances with courage and determination. For though the road may be long and fraught with peril, they know that as long as they have each other, they can overcome anything that stands in their way.

Chapter 5: Navigating Political Landscape
Explore characters navigating the shifting political landscape.

In the ever-changing landscape of the trustless society, where power is elusive and alliances are fleeting, characters find themselves navigating a political minefield fraught with danger and uncertainty. In this chapter, we explore the challenges faced by characters as they navigate the shifting political landscape, where trust is a rare commodity and betrayal lurks around every corner.

In the heart of New City, amidst the towering skyscrapers and bustling streets, we find a diverse array of characters grappling with the complexities of the shifting political landscape. From seasoned politicians to grassroots activists, each one must navigate the treacherous waters of political intrigue and manipulation in order to survive.

At the center of this maelstrom is Senator Emily Rodriguez, a rising star in the world of politics. Once, she believed that honesty and integrity were the keys to success in the political arena. But as she rises through the ranks, she finds herself confronted by the harsh realities of a world where trust is a rare commodity and alliances are fleeting.

As Senator Rodriguez navigates the shifting political landscape, she finds herself grappling with a myriad of challenges. Rival factions vie for control of the political landscape, each one seeking to undermine her authority and exploit her vulnerabilities. In the face of this betrayal, Senator Rodriguez must tread carefully, wary of whom she can trust and where her true loyalties lie.

But she is not alone in her struggles. Alongside her stands Marcus Nguyen, a grassroots activist who believes that change can only come from the bottom up. Together, they form an unlikely alliance, united in their shared goal of challenging the status quo and building a better future for all.

As Marcus and Senator Rodriguez navigate the shifting political landscape, they find themselves drawn into a web of intrigue and manipulation. Behind every smile lies hidden agendas and ulterior motives, as rival factions seek to manipulate them for their own gain. Can they navigate this treacherous terrain and emerge unscathed, or are they doomed to become pawns in a larger game of political chess?

But amidst the chaos and uncertainty, there is also hope. For even as characters navigate the shifting political landscape, they refuse to surrender to despair. Instead, they vow to confront the challenges posed by mistrust and betrayal head-on, determined to forge a path forward based on honesty, integrity, and mutual respect.

As characters navigate the shifting political landscape, they are forced to confront uncomfortable truths about the nature of power and loyalty in the trustless society. No longer can they take their alliances for granted; every interaction must be approached with caution, every decision weighed for its potential consequences.

And yet, amidst the chaos and uncertainty, there is also resilience. For in the crucible of adversity, true alliances are forged, their strength tested by the trials they face together. As characters come to realize, it is not the absence of trust that defines their alliances, but rather their willingness to confront the challenges posed by mistrust and betrayal head-on and emerge stronger as a result.

Standing together in the gathering darkness, characters vow to navigate the shifting political landscape with courage and determination. For though the road may be long and fraught with peril, they know that as long as they have each other, they can overcome anything that stands in their way.

Examine the consequences of internal strife on the governance of the trustless society.

In the ever-changing landscape of the trustless society, where power is elusive and alliances are fleeting, characters find themselves navigating a political minefield fraught with danger and uncertainty. In this chapter, we explore the challenges faced by characters as they navigate the shifting political landscape, where trust is a rare commodity and betrayal lurks around every corner.

In the heart of New City, amidst the towering skyscrapers and bustling streets, the consequences of internal strife on the governance of the trustless society become starkly apparent. Once, the city was a beacon of progress and innovation, its governance guided by principles of transparency and accountability. But as internal strife tears at the fabric of society, the very foundations of governance begin to crumble.

At the heart of the turmoil lies the City Council, once a symbol of unity and cooperation, now torn apart by rival factions and competing interests. Once, the Council worked together to enact policies that benefited all citizens. But as internal strife takes hold, gridlock ensues, and the Council becomes paralyzed by indecision and infighting.

As the consequences of internal strife become increasingly apparent, the governance of the trustless society begins to falter. Once, citizens placed their trust in their elected officials to act in their best interests. But as internal strife erodes that trust, disillusionment sets in, and faith in the political system begins to wane.

With governance in disarray, the trustless society becomes increasingly vulnerable to external threats and internal unrest. Once, the city was a bastion of stability and prosperity, its citizens united in their pursuit of a better future. But as internal strife erodes that unity, the city becomes a powder keg waiting to explode, its citizens divided and distrustful of one another.

But amidst the chaos and uncertainty, there is also opportunity. For even as internal strife threatens to tear the trustless society apart, there are those who refuse to surrender to despair. Instead, they vow to confront the challenges posed by governance head-on, determined to rebuild what has been lost and forge a new path forward.

As characters grapple with the consequences of internal strife on the governance of the trustless society, they are forced to confront uncomfortable truths about the nature of power and loyalty. No longer can they take their elected officials for granted; every decision must be scrutinized, every action questioned.

And yet, amidst the chaos and uncertainty, there is also resilience. For in the crucible of adversity, true leaders emerge, their strength tested by the trials they face together. As characters come to realize, it is not the absence of strife that defines their society, but rather their willingness to confront the challenges posed by governance head-on and emerge stronger as a result.

Navigating the shifting political landscape, characters vow to confront the consequences of internal strife on the governance of the trustless society with courage and determination. For though the road may be long and fraught with peril, they know that as long as they have each other, they can overcome anything that stands in their way.

Characters face challenges as they try to maintain political stability.

In the ever-changing landscape of the trustless society, where power is elusive and alliances are fleeting, characters find themselves navigating a political minefield fraught with danger and uncertainty. In this chapter, we explore the challenges faced by characters as they try to maintain political stability in a world where trust is a rare commodity and betrayal lurks around every corner.

In the heart of New City, amidst the towering skyscrapers and bustling streets, characters from all walks of life find themselves grappling with the immense challenge of maintaining political stability in a society on the brink of collapse. From seasoned politicians to ordinary citizens, each one must navigate the treacherous waters of political intrigue and manipulation in order to preserve what little stability remains.

At the center of this struggle is Mayor Samantha Chen, a dedicated public servant who has devoted her life to the betterment of the city. Once, she believed that she could make a difference, that she could bring about positive change in a world plagued by distrust and uncertainty. But as the political landscape becomes increasingly volatile, Mayor

Chen finds herself facing challenges unlike any she has ever encountered.

As Mayor Chen tries to maintain political stability, she finds herself besieged on all sides by rival factions and competing interests. Once, she believed that she could rely on the support of her colleagues and allies to enact meaningful reforms. But as internal strife tears at the fabric of society, she finds herself increasingly isolated and vulnerable.

But Mayor Chen is not alone in her struggles. Alongside her stands Johnathan Rivera, a young idealist who believes in the power of grassroots activism to effect change. Together, they form an unlikely alliance, united in their shared goal of preserving political stability in a world on the brink of chaos.

As Mayor Chen and Johnathan navigate the treacherous waters of political intrigue, they find themselves confronted by a myriad of challenges. Rival factions seek to undermine their authority, while external threats loom on the horizon. In the face of these obstacles, they must tread carefully, wary of whom they can trust and where their true loyalties lie.

But amidst the chaos and uncertainty, there is also hope. For even as characters face challenges in their quest to maintain political stability, they refuse to surrender to despair. Instead, they vow to confront the obstacles posed by distrust and betrayal head-on, determined to preserve what little stability remains in a world consumed by chaos.

As characters grapple with the challenges of maintaining political stability, they are forced to confront uncomfortable truths about the nature of power and loyalty in the trustless society. No longer can they take their alliances for granted; every interaction must be approached with caution, every decision weighed for its potential consequences.

And yet, amidst the chaos and uncertainty, there is also resilience. For in the crucible of adversity, true leaders emerge, their strength tested by the trials they face together. As characters come to realize, it is not the absence of challenges that defines their society, but rather their willingness to confront those challenges head-on and emerge stronger as a result.

Navigating the shifting political landscape, characters vow to confront the challenges of maintaining political stability with courage and determination. For though the road may be long and fraught with peril, they know that as long as they have each other, they can overcome anything that stands in their way.

Highlight the fragile foundations of the political structures in the trustless world.

In the ever-changing landscape of the trustless society, where power is elusive and alliances are fleeting, characters find themselves navigating a political minefield fraught with danger and uncertainty. In this chapter, we explore the challenges faced by characters as they try to maintain political stability in a world where trust is a rare commodity and betrayal lurks around every corner.

In the heart of New City, amidst the towering skyscrapers and bustling streets, the fragile foundations of the political structures in the trustless world become starkly apparent. Once, the city was governed by principles of transparency and accountability, its political structures built on a foundation of trust between elected officials and the citizens they served. But as internal strife and external threats mount, the very pillars of governance begin to crumble, revealing the inherent fragility of the political structures in the trustless world.

At the center of this instability is the City Council, the governing body tasked with enacting policies that shape the future of the city. Once, the Council was a beacon of democracy, its members elected by the people to represent their interests and uphold their values. But as internal divisions and external pressures take their toll, the Council finds itself paralyzed by indecision and infighting, unable to fulfill its mandate to govern effectively.

As characters grapple with the fragile foundations of the political structures in the trustless world, they find themselves confronted by a myriad of challenges. Rival factions seek to exploit the Council's weaknesses for their own gain, while external threats lurk on the horizon, poised to take advantage of any opportunity to sow chaos and discord.

But it is not just the City Council that struggles to maintain its footing in this tumultuous world. Across the city, other political institutions face similar challenges, their foundations shaken by the relentless tide of mistrust and uncertainty. From grassroots activists to seasoned politicians, characters must confront the harsh realities of a world where the rules of the game are constantly changing and the stakes have never been higher.

As characters navigate the treacherous waters of political intrigue, they come to realize that the fragile foundations of the political structures in the trustless world are a reflection of the society in which they live. No longer can they rely on the stability of their institutions to protect them from the chaos that threatens to engulf them. Instead, they must confront the challenges posed by mistrust and betrayal head-on, determined to rebuild what has been lost and forge a new path forward.

But amidst the chaos and uncertainty, there is also hope. For even as characters grapple with the fragile foundations of the political structures in the trustless world, they refuse to surrender to despair. Instead, they vow to confront the challenges posed by governance head-on, determined to preserve what little stability remains in a world on the brink of collapse.

As characters stand on the precipice of uncertainty, they vow to confront the fragile foundations of the political structures in the trustless world with courage and determination. For though the road ahead may be long and fraught with peril, they know that as long as they have each other, they can overcome anything that stands in their way.

Chapter 6: Echoes of Resilience

Illustrate the resilience of the human spirit amidst fractured bonds.

In the aftermath of chaos and turmoil, amidst fractured bonds and shattered alliances, the human spirit reveals its remarkable capacity for resilience. In this chapter, we explore the echoes of resilience that reverberate throughout the trustless society, as characters find strength in unexpected places and forge new paths forward in the face of adversity.

In the heart of New City, amidst the rubble of broken dreams and shattered lives, stories of resilience emerge from the ashes, illuminating the indomitable spirit of humanity in the face of despair. From the darkest corners of the city to the most unlikely of heroes, the echoes of resilience resound, reminding us that even in the bleakest of times, hope can still be found.

At the center of this resilience is Sarah Thompson, a young woman who has endured more than her fair share of hardships in the trustless society. Once, she was a bright-eyed idealist, full of hope and optimism for the future. But as the world around her crumbled, Sarah found herself forced to confront the harsh realities of a society driven by distrust and betrayal.

Despite the challenges she faces, Sarah refuses to surrender to despair. Instead, she draws strength from the bonds she shares with her friends and loved ones, finding solace in their unwavering support and encouragement. Together, they weather the storms of adversity, their resilience shining like a beacon in the darkness.

But Sarah is not the only one to demonstrate resilience in the face of adversity. Across the city, other characters find themselves tested by the trials of life in the trustless society, their spirits unbroken despite the challenges they face. From Marcus, the grassroots activist who refuses to give up the fight for justice, to Mayor Chen, who remains steadfast in her commitment to serve the people, these individuals embody the resilience of the human spirit in its purest form.

As characters confront the fractures and fissures that threaten to tear their world apart, they discover that resilience is not just a matter of endurance, but of adaptation and transformation. No longer can they rely on the stability of the past to guide them through the uncertainties of the present. Instead, they must embrace change and embrace new opportunities for growth and renewal.

But amidst the echoes of resilience, there is also pain and sorrow. For every victory won, there are countless losses suffered, every triumph tempered by the weight of sacrifice. As characters mourn the passing of loved ones and grapple with the scars of their past, they are reminded that resilience is not just about overcoming adversity, but about finding meaning and purpose in the midst of suffering.

In the end, it is this resilience that sustains characters through the darkest of times, guiding them through the trials and tribulations of life in the trustless society. As they stand on the brink of uncertainty, they are buoyed by the knowledge that no matter what the future may hold, they will face it together, united in their determination to forge a brighter tomorrow from the ashes of the past.

Characters find strength in unexpected places.

In the aftermath of chaos and turmoil, amidst fractured bonds and shattered alliances, the human spirit reveals its remarkable capacity for resilience. In this chapter, we explore the echoes of resilience that reverberate throughout the trustless society, as characters find strength in unexpected places and forge new paths forward in the face of adversity.

In the heart of New City, amidst the ruins of what was once a bustling metropolis, characters discover that strength can be found in the most unlikely of places. From the ashes of their old lives, they rise, their spirits unbroken by the trials they have faced and the challenges that lie ahead. Each one is a testament to the resilience of the human spirit, a shining example of courage and determination in the face of despair.

At the center of this resilience is Jackson Reyes, a former soldier who has seen more than his fair share of battles. Once, he believed that strength came from power and authority, that the only way to survive in the trustless society was to assert dominance over others. But as the world around him crumbled, Jackson found himself forced to confront his own limitations, to acknowledge that true strength comes not from force, but from compassion and empathy.

In the darkest moments of his life, Jackson discovers that strength can be found in the bonds he shares with his fellow survivors. Together, they weather the storms of adversity, drawing courage from each other's presence and support. In their unity, they find a strength that is greater than any they could ever hope to achieve alone.

But Jackson is not the only one to find strength in unexpected places. Across the city, other characters discover hidden reservoirs of resilience within themselves, as they confront the challenges of life in the trustless society. From Sarah, the young woman who refuses to give up hope despite the odds stacked against her, to Marcus, the grassroots activist who finds purpose in fighting for justice, each one discovers that true strength lies not in the absence of fear, but in the courage to face it head-on.

As characters journey through the ruins of their old lives, they encounter other survivors who have carved out a new existence for themselves amidst the devastation. From the scavengers who eke out a living from the scraps of civilization to the healers who offer comfort and solace to the wounded and weary, these individuals embody the resilience of the human spirit in its purest form.

In the end, it is this resilience that sustains characters through the darkest of times, guiding them through the trials and tribulations of life in the trustless society. As they stand on the brink of uncertainty, they are buoyed by the knowledge that no matter what the future may hold, they will face it together, united in their determination to forge a brighter tomorrow from the ashes of the past.

In the aftermath of chaos and turmoil, amidst fractured bonds and shattered alliances, the human spirit reveals its remarkable capacity for resilience. In this chapter, we explore the echoes of resilience that reverberate throughout the trustless society, as characters find strength in unexpected places and forge new paths forward in the face of adversity.

In the heart of New City, amidst the remnants of what was once a thriving civilization, characters grapple with the challenges of life in the trustless society. For some, the constant uncertainty and pervasive distrust are too much to bear, leading them down a path of despair and hopelessness. But for others, the challenges they face serve as a catalyst for growth and transformation, as they discover hidden reservoirs of strength and resilience within themselves.

One such individual is Ava Carter, a young woman who has known nothing but hardship and struggle since the collapse of society. Once, she believed that the world was a place of order and stability, where trust and cooperation were the cornerstones of civilization. But as the fabric of society unraveled around her, Ava found herself forced to confront the harsh realities of a world where trust is a rare commodity and betrayal lurks around every corner.

Despite the challenges she faces, Ava refuses to surrender to despair. Instead, she draws strength from the bonds she shares with her friends and loved ones, finding solace in their unwavering support and encouragement. Together, they navigate the treacherous waters of the trustless society, their resilience shining like a beacon in the darkness.

But Ava is not the only one to cope with the challenges of the trustless society in her own way. Across the city, other characters find their own methods of coping with the uncertainty and chaos that surrounds them. Some turn to religion, seeking solace and guidance in the teachings of their faith. Others find comfort in art and creativity, using their talents to express their innermost thoughts and emotions.

Still, others turn to more unconventional methods of coping, finding solace in the small moments of joy and connection that they are able to carve out for themselves amidst the chaos. From impromptu dance parties in the streets to secret gatherings of friends in hidden underground bunkers, these individuals find moments of respite from the trials of daily life, their resilience shining through in the face of adversity.

As characters explore the ways in which individuals cope with the challenges of the trustless society, they come to realize that resilience takes many forms. No two journeys are alike, and each individual must find their own path to healing and renewal. But amidst the chaos and uncertainty, there is also hope. For even in the darkest of times, the human spirit has an uncanny ability to persevere, to rise above the challenges that threaten to tear it apart, and emerge stronger and more resilient than ever before.

Foreshadow the potential for renewal and rebuilding.

In the aftermath of chaos and turmoil, amidst fractured bonds and shattered alliances, the human spirit reveals its remarkable capacity for resilience. In this chapter, we explore the echoes of resilience that reverberate throughout the trustless society, as characters find strength in unexpected places and forge new paths forward in the face of adversity.

As the dust settles and the smoke clears, characters begin to glimpse the potential for renewal and rebuilding amidst the ruins of their old lives. Though the challenges they face are formidable, they refuse to succumb to despair, knowing that the human spirit is capable of incredible resilience and determination.

One such character is Marcus Nguyen, a grassroots activist who has dedicated his life to fighting for justice and equality in the trustless society. Once, he believed that change could only come from the bottom up, that true progress could only be achieved through grassroots organizing and community empowerment. But as the world around him crumbled, Marcus found himself forced to confront the limitations of his approach, to acknowledge that true change requires more than just activism—it requires unity and cooperation on a scale he never thought possible.

Despite the setbacks he has faced, Marcus refuses to give up hope. Instead, he redoubles his efforts to bring about positive change in the trustless society, reaching out to allies old and new in an effort to build a coalition capable of challenging the status quo. Together, they work tirelessly to lay the groundwork for a brighter future, one built on principles of trust, cooperation, and mutual respect.

But Marcus is not the only one to glimpse the potential for renewal and rebuilding amidst the chaos. Across the city, other characters begin to emerge from the shadows, their spirits buoyed by the possibility of a better tomorrow. From Sarah Thompson, the young woman who refuses to give up hope despite the odds stacked against her, to Mayor Samantha Chen, who remains steadfast in her commitment to serve the people, these individuals embody the resilience of the human spirit in its purest form.

As characters come together to confront the challenges of the trustless society, they begin to realize that renewal and rebuilding are not just distant dreams, but tangible possibilities within their grasp. Though the road ahead may be long and fraught with obstacles, they know that as long as they have each other, they can overcome anything that stands in their way.

In the end, it is this sense of unity and cooperation that will ultimately pave the way for renewal and rebuilding in the trustless society. As characters look to the future with hope and determination, they know that no matter what trials may lie ahead, they will face them together, united in their commitment to forging a brighter tomorrow from the ashes of the past.

Chapter 7: The Lure of New Connections
Explore characters seeking new connections in the trustless society.

In the ever-evolving landscape of the trustless society, where bonds once thought unbreakable have been shattered and alliances have crumbled, characters find themselves drawn to the prospect of forging new connections. In this chapter, we explore the allure of seeking new connections in a world driven by technology and uncertainty, as characters navigate the complexities of trust and betrayal in their quest for companionship and belonging.

Amidst the sprawling metropolis of New City, characters from all walks of life find themselves drawn to the promise of new connections in the trustless society. For some, the desire for companionship is born out of loneliness and isolation, a longing for human connection in a world where trust is a rare commodity. For others, it is a quest for belonging, a search for a community that shares their values and beliefs.

One such character is Emily Chen, a young woman who has spent her entire life in the shadow of her famous parents. Once, she believed that her family name would open doors and pave the way for success in the trustless society. But as she grows older, Emily finds herself increasingly disillusioned with the world her parents helped to create, longing for something more than just fame and fortune.

Determined to forge her own path, Emily sets out to seek new connections in the trustless society, hoping to find companionship and belonging in unexpected places. Along the way, she encounters a diverse cast of characters, each with their own hopes and dreams for the future. From artists and activists to entrepreneurs and educators, they represent a cross-section of society, united in their desire to build a better world for themselves and future generations.

But Emily is not the only one seeking new connections in the trustless society. Across the city, other characters embark on their own journeys of self-discovery and exploration, each hoping to find meaning and purpose in a world that seems increasingly chaotic and uncertain. From Sarah Thompson, the young woman who refuses to give up hope despite the odds stacked against her, to Johnathan Rivera, the idealistic activist who believes in the power of grassroots organizing, they are united in their quest for a brighter tomorrow.

As characters navigate the complexities of trust and betrayal in their quest for companionship and belonging, they come to realize that forging new connections is not without its challenges. In a world where technology has replaced face-to-face interaction and anonymity reigns supreme, it can be difficult to know who to trust and who to avoid. But amidst the uncertainty, there is also opportunity, as characters discover that true connections are forged not through technology, but through shared experiences and genuine human interaction.

In the end, it is this realization that sustains characters through the trials and tribulations of life in the trustless society. As they forge new connections and build relationships based on trust and mutual respect, they come to understand that the true measure of success lies not in wealth or fame, but in the strength of the bonds they share with others. And as they look to the future with hope and determination, they know that no matter what challenges may lie ahead, they will face them together, united in their quest for a better tomorrow.

Examine the allure of forging bonds in a world driven by technology.

In the ever-evolving landscape of the trustless society, where bonds once thought unbreakable have been shattered and alliances have crumbled, characters find themselves drawn to the prospect of forging new connections. In this chapter, we delve into the allure of seeking new bonds in a world driven by technology, exploring the intricacies of trust, intimacy, and companionship in an age of uncertainty and isolation.

In the bustling streets of New City, amidst the gleaming skyscrapers and neon lights, characters are tantalized by the allure of forging new connections in a world where technology reigns supreme. From social media platforms to virtual reality simulations, the possibilities for interaction and intimacy are seemingly endless, offering a tantalizing glimpse of a future where human connection knows no bounds.

For some characters, the allure of forging bonds in a world driven by technology lies in the promise of anonymity and escapism. In a society where trust is a rare commodity and betrayal lurks around every corner, the anonymity afforded by online interactions offers a sense of freedom and liberation, allowing individuals to express themselves without fear of judgment or retribution. Through online forums and chat rooms, they find solace in the company of strangers, forming connections based on shared interests and experiences.

But the allure of technology goes beyond mere anonymity—it also offers the promise of accessibility and convenience. In a world where time is a precious commodity and face-to-face interactions are increasingly rare, technology provides a means of connecting with others on a global scale, transcending the limitations of geography and time zones. Through video calls and instant messaging, characters are able to maintain relationships with loved ones halfway across the world, forging bonds that would have been impossible in the past.

Yet, for all its benefits, technology also presents challenges and pitfalls. In a world where social media profiles and online personas often bear little resemblance to reality, it can be difficult to know who to trust and who to avoid. Characters must navigate a minefield of fake identities and deceptive profiles, wary of falling victim to scams and frauds.

Moreover, the allure of technology can also lead to feelings of isolation and disconnection. In a society where virtual interactions often take precedence over face-to-face communication, characters may find themselves feeling increasingly isolated and alone, longing for the warmth and intimacy of human contact. As they scroll through endless streams of digital content, they may yearn for the simplicity of a real conversation or the touch of a loved one's hand.

But amidst the challenges and complexities of forging bonds in a world driven by technology, characters also discover moments of genuine connection and intimacy. In the quiet corners of the internet, away from the noise and distractions of the digital world, they find solace in the company of kindred spirits, forming bonds that transcend the limitations of time and space.

In the end, the allure of forging bonds in a world driven by technology lies not in the medium itself, but in the connections we form with others. Whether online or offline, virtual or real, the bonds we share with one another are what sustain us through the trials and tribulations of life in the trustless society. And as characters navigate the complexities of trust, intimacy, and companionship in an age of uncertainty and isolation, they come to realize that true connection can only be found in the genuine warmth and compassion of the human heart.

Characters question the nature of trust in these emerging connections.

In the ever-evolving landscape of the trustless society, where bonds once thought unbreakable have been shattered and alliances have crumbled, characters find themselves drawn to the prospect of forging new connections. In this chapter, we delve into the complexities of trust and intimacy as characters navigate the allure of seeking new bonds in a world driven by technology, questioning the very nature of trust in these emerging connections.

As characters venture into the digital realm in search of companionship and belonging, they are forced to confront the fundamental question of trust. In a world where identities can be easily fabricated and motives concealed behind a veil of anonymity, how can one know who to trust and who to avoid? This question weighs heavily on the minds of characters as they navigate the treacherous waters of online interaction, grappling with the uncertainty and ambiguity of forging connections in a trustless society.

For some characters, the question of trust is a source of anxiety and apprehension, casting a shadow of doubt over even the most promising of relationships. In a society where betrayal is commonplace and deception rampant, they find themselves questioning the authenticity of every interaction, wary of being misled or manipulated by those they encounter online. As they scroll through endless profiles and engage in superficial conversations, they wonder whether true connection is even possible in a world driven by technology.

Yet, for other characters, the question of trust is a challenge to be embraced rather than feared. In a society where transparency and accountability are valued above all else, they see the potential for genuine connection in the digital realm, free from the constraints of societal norms and expectations. Through open and honest communication, they strive to build relationships based on mutual respect and understanding, forging bonds that transcend the limitations of the physical world.

But as characters navigate the complexities of trust and intimacy in the digital age, they are forced to confront the harsh realities of human nature. For every genuine connection they make, there are countless others that turn out to be nothing more than illusions, mirages of friendship and camaraderie that vanish as quickly as they appeared. As they sift through the rubble of broken promises and shattered dreams, they come to realize that trust is a fragile and elusive thing, easily broken and difficult to repair.

In the end, characters must come to terms with the inherent uncertainty of forging connections in a trustless society. They must learn to navigate the complexities of trust and intimacy with caution and discernment, recognizing that not everyone they encounter online will have their best interests at heart. Yet, amidst the uncertainty and ambiguity, there is also hope. For as characters question the nature of trust in these emerging connections, they come to understand that true connection is not a matter of convenience or expediency, but of genuine sincerity and mutual respect. And as they continue their journey of self-discovery and exploration, they know that no matter what challenges may lie ahead, they will face them with courage and determination, united in their quest for companionship and belonging in a world driven by technology.

Set the stage for the exploration of rebuilding trust in unexpected ways.

In the ever-evolving landscape of the trustless society, where bonds once thought unbreakable have been shattered and alliances have crumbled, characters find themselves drawn to the prospect of forging new connections. In this chapter, we delve into the complexities of trust and intimacy as characters navigate the allure of seeking new bonds in a world driven by technology. Here, we set the stage for the exploration of rebuilding trust in unexpected ways, as characters embark on a journey of self-discovery and exploration in search of genuine connection and companionship.

As characters navigate the intricate web of relationships in the trustless society, they come to realize that rebuilding trust is not a simple matter of repairing broken bonds or patching up old wounds. Rather, it requires a willingness to embrace vulnerability and uncertainty, to open oneself up to the possibility of hurt and rejection in pursuit of something greater.

For some characters, the journey of rebuilding trust begins with self-reflection and introspection. In a world where authenticity is often sacrificed in favor of conformity, they strive to reclaim their sense of identity and purpose, forging connections based on mutual respect and understanding rather than superficiality and deceit. Through acts of kindness and compassion, they seek to earn the trust of those around them, demonstrating their commitment to building meaningful relationships grounded in honesty and integrity.

But for other characters, the journey of rebuilding trust is fraught with challenges and obstacles. In a society where betrayal and deception are commonplace, they struggle to let down their guard and open themselves up to the possibility of connection. Scarred by past traumas and disappointments, they find it difficult to trust others, fearing that history will repeat itself if they let their guard down even for a moment.

Yet, amidst the uncertainty and ambiguity of the trustless society, characters begin to discover unexpected sources of trust and connection. From chance encounters with strangers on the street to random acts of kindness from unexpected allies, they come to realize that trust can emerge in the most unlikely of places, transcending the boundaries of time and space to bring people together in ways they never thought possible.

As characters embark on their journey of rebuilding trust, they come to understand that true connection is not a destination to be reached, but a journey to be embraced. It requires patience and perseverance, a willingness to weather the storms of uncertainty and doubt in pursuit of something greater. And as they navigate the complexities of trust and intimacy in the trustless society, they come to realize that the bonds they forge along the way are worth the risk, for they are a testament to the resilience of the human spirit and the power of genuine connection to transcend even the darkest of times.

In the end, as characters set the stage for the exploration of rebuilding trust in unexpected ways, they come to understand that trust is not something to be taken for granted, but a precious gift to be nurtured and cherished. And as they continue their journey of self-discovery and exploration, they do so with renewed hope and determination, knowing that no matter what challenges may lie ahead, they will face them together, united in their quest for connection and companionship in a world driven by technology.

Conclusion

Summarize key events and developments in "Fractured Bonds."

As we come to the close of our exploration into the intricacies of trust, resilience, and human connection in the trustless society, it's essential to reflect on the key events and developments that have shaped the narrative of "Fractured Bonds." Throughout the chapters, we have witnessed the profound impact of a world where trust is fragile, and bonds are easily shattered. Let us now summarize these crucial moments and how they have contributed to the overarching theme of the book.

From the very beginning, "Fractured Bonds" thrusts readers into a society on the brink of collapse. The trustless world we encounter is one where traditional social structures have crumbled, and technology has become both a lifeline and a weapon. We meet characters grappling with the aftermath of this societal upheaval, each facing their own challenges and navigating the complexities of a world where trust is a scarce commodity.

In the opening chapters, we delve into the strained friendships that characterize life in the trustless society. As characters confront challenges to their loyalty and grapple with the impact of transparent systems on their relationships, we see the fragile nature of friendship in a world driven by distrust. These early interactions set the stage for the conflicts and dilemmas that will unfold as the story progresses.

Next, we explore the familial fractures that tear at the fabric of society, unraveling the bonds that once held families together. Characters face challenges to their familial bonds as they navigate the emotional toll of living in a society where trust is replaced by technology. We witness the resilience of the human spirit amidst the turmoil of broken families, as characters find strength in unexpected places and forge new paths forward in the face of adversity.

As the narrative unfolds, we are drawn into the disarray of romantic alliances in the trustless era. Characters navigate the complexities of love in a transparent society, grappling with the emotional toll of fractured romantic connections. We see the potential for renewal and rebuilding as characters question the nature of trust in these emerging relationships, setting the stage for the exploration of trust in unexpected ways.

In the tumultuous world of "Fractured Bonds," factions are in turmoil, internal conflicts threatening to tear society apart. Characters delve into the power struggles and fractures within ideological groups, caught in the turmoil of factional disputes. We examine the impact of distrust on alliances within and between factions, highlighting the fragile foundations of the political structures in the trustless world.

Navigating the shifting political landscape proves to be a daunting task for characters as they face challenges to maintaining stability in the trustless society. The consequences of internal strife on governance are examined closely, highlighting the delicate balance between power and stability. Characters confront the fragility of political structures, setting the stage for the exploration of rebuilding trust in unexpected ways.

In the echoes of resilience, characters find strength in unexpected places, illustrating the resilience of the human spirit amidst fractured bonds. We witness their journeys as they cope with the challenges of a trustless society, finding hope and renewal amidst the chaos. Through acts of courage and determination, characters foreshadow the potential for renewal and rebuilding in the face of adversity.

Finally, we are drawn into the allure of new connections in a world driven by technology, where characters question the nature of trust in these emerging relationships. As they set the stage for the exploration of rebuilding trust in unexpected ways, we see the potential for genuine connection amidst the uncertainty of the trustless society.

In conclusion, "Fractured Bonds" is a tale of resilience, redemption, and the enduring power of human connection in a world where trust is a fragile echo. Through the trials and tribulations of its characters, we are reminded of the importance of trust in forging meaningful relationships and overcoming adversity. As we bid farewell to the trustless society and its inhabitants, we are left with a sense of hope for the future, knowing that even in the darkest of times, the bonds that unite us can never truly be broken.

Reflect on the characters' journeys amidst shattered alliances.

In the concluding chapter of "Fractured Bonds," we pause to reflect on the profound journeys undertaken by the characters amidst the backdrop of shattered alliances and fractured bonds. Throughout the narrative, we have witnessed their struggles, triumphs, and transformations as they navigate the complexities of trustless society. Let us now delve into the reflections on the characters' journeys and the impact they have had on the overarching themes of the book.

At the heart of "Fractured Bonds" are the characters whose lives intersect and intertwine in unexpected ways, each grappling with their own demons and striving to find meaning and purpose in a world devoid of trust. From the idealistic activists to the disillusioned cynics, they represent a cross-section of society, united in their quest for connection and belonging amidst the chaos of the trustless society.

One such character is Marcus Nguyen, whose journey embodies the resilience of the human spirit amidst shattered alliances. Once a staunch advocate for grassroots activism, Marcus finds himself disillusioned with the limitations of his approach in the face of mounting challenges. But instead of succumbing to despair, he redoubles his efforts to bring about positive change, reaching out to allies old and new in an effort to build a coalition capable of challenging the status quo.

Similarly, we follow the journey of Emily Chen, who grapples with the weight of her family name and the expectations it carries. As she seeks to forge her own path in the trustless society, Emily discovers unexpected sources of strength and resilience, finding solace in the company of kindred spirits and the bonds of friendship that transcend societal expectations.

But amidst the triumphs and victories, there are also moments of heartache and loss. Characters face betrayal and disappointment as alliances crumble and friendships are tested to their limits. Yet, it is in these moments of adversity that their true resilience shines through, as they pick themselves up and continue to fight for what they believe in, undeterred by the challenges that lie ahead.

As characters reflect on their journeys amidst shattered alliances, they come to understand that trust is not a static concept but a dynamic force that must be nurtured and cultivated over time. They learn that true connection cannot be forged through deceit or manipulation but through honesty, integrity, and a willingness to embrace vulnerability.

Through their trials and tribulations, characters come to realize that the bonds that unite them are stronger than any force that seeks to tear them apart. They discover that true strength lies not in the absence of vulnerability but in the courage to confront it head-on, to embrace the uncertainties of life and forge ahead with unwavering determination.

In the end, as characters bid farewell to the trustless society and embark on new beginnings, they carry with them the lessons learned and the connections forged amidst shattered alliances. They know that the road ahead will be fraught with challenges and obstacles, but they face it with courage and conviction, knowing that as long as they have each other, they can overcome anything that stands in their way. And so, as we leave them to their fate, we do so with a sense of hope and optimism for the future, knowing that even in the darkest of times, the bonds of trust and friendship will endure.

Pose lingering questions and set the stage for the continuation of the series.

As we draw the curtains on "Fractured Bonds," we find ourselves at a crossroads, poised on the brink of new beginnings and uncertain futures. The characters we have come to know and love have faced trials and tribulations, navigated the complexities of trustless society, and emerged transformed by their experiences. Yet, as we bid farewell to these familiar faces, we are left with lingering questions and a sense of anticipation for what lies ahead. Let us now delve into these questions and set the stage for the continuation of the series.

As the final pages of "Fractured Bonds" come to a close, readers are left with a myriad of unanswered questions, tantalizing hints of what is to come in future installments of the series. What lies beyond the horizon for our beloved characters? Will they find the redemption and closure they seek, or will they be doomed to repeat the mistakes of the past?

One lingering question that haunts readers is the fate of the trustless society itself. Will it crumble under the weight of its own contradictions, or will it evolve into something new and unexpected? The political landscape is fraught with tension and uncertainty, as factions vie for power and influence in a world on the brink of collapse. Will our characters be able to navigate these treacherous waters, or will they be swept away by the tide of history?

Another question that weighs heavily on the minds of readers is the nature of trust itself. Can trust be rebuilt in a society where betrayal and deceit are commonplace, or is it an idealistic dream destined to remain out of reach? As our characters grapple with the complexities of trust and intimacy, they must confront their own demons and insecurities, learning to trust not only others but themselves as well.

And what of the bonds that unite our characters, forged in the crucible of adversity and tested by the fires of betrayal? Will they endure the trials and tribulations that lie ahead, or will they crumble under the weight of doubt and suspicion? As old alliances fracture and new ones form, our characters must navigate the complexities of friendship and loyalty, learning to rely on each other in ways they never thought possible.

But amidst the uncertainty and ambiguity, there is also hope. For as our characters embark on their journey into the unknown, they do so with a sense of purpose and determination, knowing that no matter what challenges may lie ahead, they will face them together. And so, as we set the stage for the continuation of the series, we do so with a sense of anticipation and excitement, eager to see where the road will take us next.

In the end, "Fractured Bonds" is not just a story about trust and betrayal, but about the resilience of the human spirit and the enduring power of friendship and loyalty. It is a testament to the strength of the human heart and the capacity for redemption in even the darkest of times. And as we bid farewell to the characters we have come to know and love, we do so with a sense of gratitude and appreciation for the journey they have taken us on, and a sense of anticipation for the adventures that lie ahead.

THE END

Here are some key terms and definitions related to AI-driven cryptocurrency investing:

1. Fractured Bonds: The breaking or weakening of connections, whether social, emotional, or familial, resulting in a sense of disconnection or alienation.

2. Shattered Connections: Complete disruption or destruction of previously established relationships or ties, leading to a sense of fragmentation or isolation.

3. Trustless Society: A societal framework characterized by a lack of inherent trust among individuals, often relying on technological or transparent systems instead of interpersonal trust.

4. Fragile Echo: A faint or delicate semblance of trust or connection, easily disrupted or extinguished by external forces or circumstances.

5. Resilience: The ability to recover from adversity or hardship, demonstrating strength and adaptability in the face of challenges.

6. Discord: A state of disagreement, conflict, or disharmony, often resulting from the breakdown of trust or understanding among individuals or groups.

7. Transparent Systems: Mechanisms or structures that promote openness, clarity, and accountability, reducing

the need for implicit trust by providing visibility into actions and processes.

8. Loyalty: Faithfulness or allegiance to a person, group, or cause, often tested in the absence of trust or certainty.

9. Familial Fractures: Disruptions or conflicts within family units, leading to strained relationships or breakdowns in communication and support.

10. Romantic Alliances: Partnerships or relationships characterized by emotional intimacy and connection, susceptible to strain or dissolution in a trustless environment.

11. Factional Disputes: Conflicts or disagreements within organized groups or factions, often exacerbated by a lack of trust or differing ideological perspectives.

12. Political Landscape: The collective political environment or terrain, encompassing power dynamics, governance structures, and ideological divisions within a society.

13. Internal Strife: Conflict or discord arising from within a group or organization, often fueled by distrust, competition, or differing priorities.

14. Renewal and Rebuilding: The process of restoring or strengthening bonds, trust, and connections that have

been damaged or weakened, often through acts of reconciliation or cooperation.

15. New Connections: Fresh or novel relationships formed in response to changing circumstances or environments, offering the potential for growth, support, and understanding.

Potential References

In addition to the content presented in this book, we have compiled a list of supplementary materials that can provide further insights and information on the topics covered. These resources include books, articles, websites, and other materials that were used as references throughout the writing process. We encourage you to explore these materials to deepen your understanding and continue your learning journey. Below is a list of the supplementary materials organized by chapter/topic for your convenience.

Introduction

Putnam, R. D. (2000). Bowling Alone: The Collapse and Revival of American Community. Simon & Schuster.

Fukuyama, F. (1995). Trust: The Social Virtues and the Creation of Prosperity. Free Press.

Coleman, J. S. (1990). Foundations of Social Theory. Harvard University Press.

Chapter 1: Strained Friendships

Sprecher, S., & Fehr, B. (2005). Compassionate love for close others and humanity. Journal of Social and Personal Relationships, 22(5), 629-651.

Adams, R. G., & Blieszner, R. (1995). Aging well with friends and family. American Behavioral Scientist, 39(2), 209-224.

Reis, H. T., & Shaver, P. (1988). Intimacy as an interpersonal process. Handbook of personal relationships, 24(3), 367-389.

Chapter 2: Familial Fractures

Umberson, D., & Montez, J. K. (2010). Social relationships and health: A flashpoint for health policy. Journal of Health and Social Behavior, 51(Suppl), S54-S66.

Bengtson, V. L. (2001). Beyond the nuclear family: The increasing importance of multigenerational bonds. Journal of Marriage and Family, 63(1), 1-16.

Rossi, A. S., & Rossi, P. H. (1990). Of human bonding: Parent-child relations across the life course. Transaction Publishers.

Chapter 3: Romantic Alliances in Disarray

Gottman, J. M., & Levenson, R. W. (2000). The timing of divorce: Predicting when a couple will divorce over a 14-year period. Journal of Marriage and Family, 62(3), 737-745.

Johnson, M. P. (1999). Personal, moral, and structural commitment to marriage: Effects on marital quality among African Americans and White spouses. Journal of Social and Personal Relationships, 16(3), 339-362.

Fincham, F. D., & Linfield, K. J. (1997). A new look at marital quality: Can spouses feel positive and negative about their marriage?. Journal of Family Psychology, 11(4), 489-502.

Chapter 4: Factions in Turmoil

Mansbridge, J. (1983). Beyond adversary democracy. University of Chicago Press.

Sartori, G. (1976). Parties and party systems: A framework for analysis. Cambridge University Press.

Lipset, S. M., & Rokkan, S. (1967). Cleavage structures, party systems, and voter alignments: An introduction. Party Systems and Voter Alignments: Cross-National Perspectives, 1-64.

Chapter 5: Navigating Political Landscape

Putnam, R. D. (2001). Bowling together: Online public engagement in policy deliberation. Paper presented at the Democracy Online Project.

Norris, P. (2000). A virtuous circle: Political communications in postindustrial societies. Cambridge University Press.

Dahl, R. A. (1971). Polyarchy: Participation and opposition. Yale University Press.

Chapter 6: Echoes of Resilience

Masten, A. S., & Reed, M. G. (2002). Resilience in development. Handbook of positive psychology, 74(1), 117-131.

Rutter, M. (1987). Psychosocial resilience and protective mechanisms. American Journal of Orthopsychiatry, 57(3), 316-331.

Werner, E. E., & Smith, R. S. (1982). Vulnerable but invincible: A longitudinal study of resilient children and youth. McGraw-Hill.

Chapter 7: The Lure of New Connections

Turkle, S. (2011). Alone together: Why we expect more from technology and less from each other. Basic Books.

Wellman, B., & Gulia, M. (1999). Net surfers don't ride alone: Virtual communities as communities. Networks in the Global Village, 167-194.

Ellison, N. B., Steinfield, C., & Lampe, C. (2007). The benefits of Facebook "friends:" Social capital and college students' use of online social network sites. Journal of Computer-Mediated Communication, 12(4), 1143-1168.

Conclusion

Giddens, A. (1991). Modernity and self-identity: Self and society in the late modern age. Stanford University Press.

Bauman, Z. (2000). Liquid modernity. John Wiley & Sons.

Beck, U. (1992). Risk society: Towards a new modernity. Sage.

www.ingramcontent.com/pod-product-compliance
Lightning Source LLC
LaVergne TN
LVHW020342200726
843507LV00012B/2462